GRAPHIC LIBRARY

DISASTERS IN HISTORY

THE DONNER PARTY

by Scott R. Welvaert

illustrated by Ron Frenz and
Charles Barnett III

Consultant:
Kristin Johnson, Librarian
Salt Lake Community College
Salt Lake City, Utah
Editor, *Unfortunate Emigrants: Narratives
of the Donner Party*

Capstone *press*

Mankato, Minnesota

Graphic Library is published by Capstone Press,
151 Good Counsel Drive, P.O. Box 669, Mankato, Minnesota 56002.
www.capstonepress.com

1 2 3 4 5 6 11 10 09 08 07 06

Library of Congress Cataloging-in-Publication Data
Welvaert, Scott R.
   The Donner Party / by Scott Welvaert; illustrated by Ron Frenz and Charles Barnett III.
   p. cm.—(Graphic library. Disasters in history)
   Summary: "In graphic novel format, tells the story of the Donner Party's struggle to reach
California despite harsh weather and starvation"—Provided by publisher.
   Includes bibliographical references and index.
   ISBN-13: 978-0-7368-5479-5 (hardcover)
   ISBN-10: 0-7368-5479-7 (hardcover)
   ISBN-13: 978-0-7368-6874-7 (softcover pbk.)
   ISBN-10: 0-7368-6874-7 (softcover pbk.)
   1. Donner Party—Juvenile literature. 2. Pioneers—California—Biography—Juvenile
literature. 3. Pioneers—West (U.S.)—Biography—Juvenile literature. 4. Overland journeys to the
Pacific—Juvenile literature. 5. Frontier and pioneer life—West (U.S.)—Juvenile literature.
I. Frenz, Ron, ill. II. Barnett, Charles, III, ill. III. Title. IV. Series.
F868.N5W415 2006
978'.02 2 22   2005031301

Art Director
Jason Knudson

Graphic Designers
Bob Lentz and Thomas Emery

Production Artist
Alison Thiele

Storyboard Artist
Jason Knudson

Colorist
Benjamin Hunzeker

Editor
Christine Peterson

Editor's note: Direct quotations from primary sources are indicated by a yellow background.

Direct quotations appear on the following pages:
Page 4, from a letter written by Tamsen Donner dated May, 11, 1846 (http://members.aol.com/
   DanMRosen/donner/may46.htm).
Page 12, from *The Expedition of the Donner Party and its Tragic Fate* by Eliza P. Donner
   Houghton (Chicago: A. C. McClurg & Co., 1911).
Page 18, from Mary Graves' account of Forlorn Hope as published in *History of the Donner
   Party, A Tragedy of the Sierra* by C. F. McGlashan, (Stanford University, California:
   Stanford University Press, 1940).
Page 24, from a statement given by Donner Party rescuer Daniel Rhoads in 1873 (http://www.
   geocities.com/Heartland/Ranch/5417/GenReports/DanielR.htm#bancroft).

Table of Contents

CHAPTER 1
CHASING A DREAM

In the 1840s, thousands of Americans left their homes and businesses in the east and headed west to California. In May 1846, a group of emigrants left Independence, Missouri, bound for California. Along the way, they were joined by more emigrants, forming a group of 87 people and 23 wagons. This group would become known as the Donner Party.

George Donner and his wife, Tamsen, had a large farm in Illinois. But they were attracted to the free land in California.

There's plenty of rich farmland in California.

I have no doubt it will be an advantage to our children and to us.

It'll take a lot of work to travel 1,600 miles before fall.

At first, traveling was easy. The trail followed rivers as it crossed the plains. There was water to drink and plenty of wild game to eat.

Virginia, what do you suppose California is like?

I'm not sure, Elitha. My father says it's warm and sunny there all the time.

Just ahead of the Donner Party, Lansford Hastings was telling other emigrants about a new, shorter route to California. But Hastings had never traveled his cutoff with wagons.

My cutoff is faster and easier than the usual trail. We're sure to be in California before winter.

After two months, the Donner Party had crossed Kansas and Nebraska territories.

In late June 1846, the Donner Party arrived in Fort Laramie, Wyoming. At the fort, Reed met a mountain man who had followed Hastings Cutoff.

We've been reading about a shortcut to California.

I just took the cutoff back from California. You'll never get your wagons through.

You'd be better off taking the old route.

The emigrants decided to rest at Fort Laramie.

We're wasting time resting here for two days. It's still a long way to California.

Yes, but if we overwork the oxen, we won't make it to California.

The 59 emigrants at Truckee Lake needed shelters. Louis Keseberg and his wife Philipine struggled to build a small shack.

We need to get this shack finished before the next storm hits.

I hope these logs can stand up to the snow and winds.

Six miles away, the Donner families were also making camp.

Take the wagon covers to make our tent stronger.

Take these quilts too.

For the next six weeks, 81 emigrants of the Donner Party remained trapped in the mountains. Many of their animals got lost in the storms and were buried in the snow.

By mid-December, the emigrants had killed their remaining animals for food. Most people were weak, ill, and starving. One person had died from starvation.

The cries of hunger from my brothers and sisters are more than I can stand.

We have to go for help.

As December ended, the remaining snowshoers realized they had no other choice. They decided to eat the dead.

By January 1847, the snowshoers had been away from Truckee Lake for almost a month. Eight people had died along the way.

How far do you think we have left?

I don't know. I'm starting to believe there is no end to these mountains.

On January 18, the survivors found a small ranch, just outside the mountains.

What's happened to these poor people?

They're starving. Get them some food. Hurry!

By March 19, a third relief party had come and gone at the other camps. Tamsen Donner again decided to stay with her husband. A few days later, George Donner died. Only two survivors remained.

Mrs. Donner, it's the only way. There's nothing left. If we eat human meat, we will live.

I would rather die than resort to such a gruesome act!

Then you are sealing your fate.

Days later, Tamsen Donner died of starvation.

By April 21, 1847, the last relief party reached the camp at Truckee Lake. They led the last survivor out of the mountains.

The Donner Party's long and terrible journey west was finally over.

MORE ABOUT THE DONNER PARTY

The Donner Party consisted of 87 people and 23 wagons. Only 29 of the 87 people in the Donner Party were men, age 15 or older. The rest were women and children.

In all, 41 people died during the Donner Party's journey to California. Thirty-six people died in the mountains during the winter. Of those who died, 32 were male and nine were female.

When the snow buried the cattle in the mountains, the emigrants used poles with bent nails on the end to search the snow for them.

Washoe Indians brought a small amount of roots to the Breen family while they were trapped in the mountains.

The group of snowshoers later became known as the Forlorn Hope.

Four relief parties went into the Sierra Nevada to rescue the Donner Party. Forlorn Hope survivors William Eddy and William Foster volunteered to join the third relief party that went to the Donner Party camps.

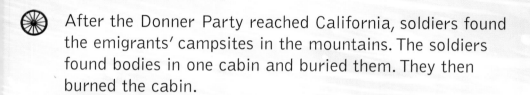 After the Donner Party reached California, soldiers found the emigrants' campsites in the mountains. The soldiers found bodies in one cabin and buried them. They then burned the cabin.

Parts of the Sierra Nevada have been renamed for the Donner Party. Truckee Lake is now called Donner Lake. The mountain summit is called Donner Summit. The rocky path over the summit is named Donner Pass.

In 2004, scientists found the location of the Donner camp near Alder Creek. Scientists dug up objects including bits of china, jewelry, pieces of bone, and a cooking hearth. Scientists are testing the bones to see if they are animal or human.

After she arrived in California, Virginia Reed wrote her cousin and offered this advice about traveling west: "Never take no cutoffs and hurry along as fast as you can."

GLOSSARY

banish (BAN-ish)—to send someone away from a place and order the person never to return

cannibalism (KAN-uh-buh-liz-uhm)—the act of a human eating human flesh

cutoff (KUHT-of)—a shorter route than the one usually taken

emigrants (EM-uh-grantz)—people who have left their homes in search of new ones

relief party (ri-LEEF PAR-tee)—a group of people who try to save trapped people

INTERNET SITES

FactHound offers a safe, fun way to find Internet sites related to this book. All of the sites on FactHound have been researched by our staff.

Here's how:

1. *Visit www.facthound.com*
2. Type in this special code **0736854797** for age-appropriate sites. Or enter a search word related to this book for a more general search.
3. Click on the **Fetch It** button.

FactHound will fetch the best sites for you!

READ MORE

Bryant, Jill. *Wagon Train.* Real Life Stories. Mankato, Minn.: Weigl, 2003.

Calabro, Marian. *The Perilous Journey of the Donner Party.* New York: Clarion, 1999.

Rau, Dana Meachen. *The Life on the Oregon Trail.* Daily Life. San Diego: Kidhaven Press, 2002.

Wachtel, Roger. *The Donner Party.* Cornerstones of Freedom. New York: Children's Press, 2003.

BIBLIOGRAPHY

Houghton, Eliza Donner. *The Expedition of the Donner Party and its Tragic Fate.* Chicago: A. C. McClurg & Co., 1911.

Johnson, Kristin. *New Light on the Donner Party.* (http://www.utahcrossroads.org/DonnerParty).

Johnson, Kristin. *Unfortunate Emigrants: Narratives of the Donner Party.* Logan, Utah: Utah State University Press, 1996.

McGlashan, C. F. *History of the Donner Party: A Tragedy of the Sierra.* Stanford, Calif.: Stanford University Press, 1940.

INDEX